Over London

Photography by HEATHER HOOK

Visitors to London are fortunate to be able to enjoy the views from many different angles – from street level, from the river, even from underground. But one of the most exciting ways to admire the landscape is from the sky, so here we bring you a special bird's-eye view of London with stunning all-new full-colour photographs. Included is everything from the best-loved historic sites to modern-day sporting venues – and we travel a short distance beyond the city itself to take in the iconic Hampton Court Palace, Kew Gardens, Windsor Castle and Eton College.

When the Romans founded the city of Londinium almost 2,000 years ago, they would have found it difficult to imagine the metropolis it has become, with Greater London covering an area of more than 1,500 square kilometres (600 square miles).

For centuries London grew up within the Roman walls, but after the Great Fire of London of 1666 it began to develop beyond the walls. The following centuries saw villages and countryside swallowed up as London grew, but even in Georgian times the city was surrounded by fields and market gardens.

The growth of the British Empire, along with the Industrial Revolution, saw an explosion of development: the docks, the railways, the migration of people into the city – and subsequent housing – transformed the landscape. In the 21st century, while relishing and preserving its heritage, England's capital continues to look to the future and grow, with changes to the skyline and the building of fabulous new facilities, including those of a nation proud to welcome sporting heroes in 2012, and The Shard which opened to the public in 2013.

Gill Knappett

Love London? See it from a different view.

Queen Elizabeth Olympic Park

*L*ondon's eastern skyline underwent a spectacular transformation with the construction of the **Olympic Park** at Stratford.

This photograph, taken during construction of the amazing site, shows: the **Olympic Stadium** (centre of main photograph), set in a bowl in the ground; the **Velodrome** with its curved roof (foreground of inset photograph) and the rectangular **Basketball Arena** beyond, overlooked by the **Olympic and Paralympic Village** – the tall, apartment-style buildings. Also seen in the inset photograph are the colourful **Riverbank Arena** pitches (front right) and the wave-like roof of the **Aquatics Centre**, left of the main stadium.

The striking red steel structure is ***ArcelorMittal Orbit***, an artwork by Anish Kapoor, towering 115-m (377-feet) high; visitors can ride to the top in a lift for views over the park and beyond.

With a theme on sustainability, some other venues in the capital also became part of the 2012 Games, including **Wembley Stadium** and **Wembley Arena**, **Wimbledon's All England Club**, **Lord's Cricket Ground**, the **O2 Arena** – and even **Horse Guards Parade**.

Beyond the 2012 Games, development of the park – now Queen Elizabeth Olympic Park – leaves a lasting legacy, providing new housing, cafés and bars as well as sporting venues, with a backdrop reflecting Britain's centuries-old passion for green, open spaces.

Past glories: 1908 and 1948

Having hosted the event twice before, in 2012 London became the first city to host the modern Games three times. White City Stadium was the venue in 1908, when Edwardian Britain changed the length of the marathon from its then-customary 25 miles (40kms) so that it could start at Windsor Castle (specifically beneath the windows of the royal nursery at the request of Princess Mary, wife of the Prince of Wales). The finish line at the stadium was even moved so that the race ended in front of King Edward VII.

The 1948 London Games were a relatively low-key affair, nicknamed the 'Austerity Games' in view of the post-Second World War economic climate and continued rationing. In those simpler times the crowds were thrilled at an opening ceremony attended by King George VI, when 2,500 pigeons were set free as the flag was raised, the Royal Horse Artillery sounded a 21-gun salute, and in his opening speech Lord Burghley spoke of a 'warm flame of hope for a better understanding in the world which has burned so low'.

Greenwich

The **Royal Borough of Greenwich** was granted its royal status in 2012. Fronting the River Thames in the heart of Greenwich is the former **Royal Naval College**, designed by Christopher Wren and a fine example of symmetrical architecture. A royal palace – the birthplace of Henry VIII and Elizabeth I – stood here before a hospital for disabled seamen was built in the early 18th century, which then served as the Royal Naval College from 1873 to 1998. Today it houses the **University of Greenwich**, **Trinity College of Music** and, in **Pepys House**, the **Discover Greenwich Visitor Centre** and **Greenwich Tourist Information Centre**.

Alongside the river, the mid 19th-century tea clipper ***Cutty Sark*** stands in dry dock. Although severely damaged by fire in 2007, an extensive restoration programme means that this much-loved attraction can be visited once more in Cutty Sark Gardens.

The building in the centre of the main photograph is the **National Maritime Museum**. Founded in 1934, it comprises the museum itself, **The Queen's House** and the **Royal Observatory**. The National Maritime Museum is a magnificent celebration of Britain's sea-going heritage, with impressive art galleries and vast collections of exhibits. A colonnaded walkway leads to The Queen's House, designed by Inigo Jones for Anne of Denmark (wife of James I) who did not live to see its completion.

Beyond this is **Greenwich Park**. Created as a royal park in 1433, it is now home to the Royal Observatory (see inset photograph) where the Prime Meridian has served as the world's measure for time since 1884. Left of the dome of the Royal Observatory is **Flamsteed House**; the red 'time ball' which falls every day at 13.00 GMT can be seen at the top of the Octagon Room.

Next to the Royal Observatory, a statue of General James Wolfe stands at the head of tree-lined Blackheath Avenue, which leads to Blackheath beyond.

Canary Wharf and the O2 Arena

Over the water from **Greenwich** lies **Canary Wharf** on the Isle of Dogs, where wharves and warehouses of a bygone era have given way to gleaming office buildings, riverside apartments, shopping malls, wine bars, restaurants and works of art on public display.

Canary Wharf is part of London's **Docklands**, the building of which began on the River Thames in 1802, relieving the congestion on the quays further downriver, and leading to this becoming the world's largest port. But new technologies and the development of container ships led to the area's steady decline and eventual closure in the 20th century.

A huge redevelopment programme during the 1980s–90s saw a regeneration of what had become a derelict part of the East End, with new businesses attracted to the area and the introduction of new transport links, including the Docklands Light Railway and an extension of the Jubilee Line.

As expansion has continued, alongside the sky-high buildings the dockside retains a certain charm at West India Quay, where the **Museum of London Docklands** enables visitors to explore the history of the Port of London.

The O2 Arena

The domed **O2 Arena**, designed by Richard Rogers, caused much comment when it first opened on 31 December 1999 as the Millennium Dome. The public was able to visit the Dome during the whole of 2000, when the millennium year was celebrated with high-tech entertainments and circus-style performances held daily.

Reconstruction work started in 2003, and in 2007 the O2 Arena opened as an entertainment complex. With state-of-the-art facilities, and excellent transport links by rail and river, this is one of Europe's largest and busiest venues for concerts, shows, exhibitions and sporting events.

Tower of London

Overlooking the River Thames is the **Tower of London**, which in its time has been a fortress, a royal residence, a prison, an armoury, a mint, an observatory – and even a menagerie. Today it is a popular tourist attraction, not least because of the Yeoman Warders, resplendent in their distinctive uniforms, who have guarded the tower since the 15th century. The **White Tower** at the centre of the Inner Ward was the original 'tower', started in the 11th century by William the Conqueror. Within the boundaries of the Tower of London is the **Bloody Tower**, where the boy-king Edward V and his brother were imprisoned in 1483, and **Waterloo Barracks**, home to the **Jewel House** where the Crown Jewels are displayed.

An entrance leading from the river to the tower is known as Traitors' Gate, through which prisoners were once delivered to their fate. Anne Boleyn, Henry VIII's second wife, arrived by boat to be executed on **Tower Green** in 1536 – where a similar end met Catherine Howard, Henry's fifth wife, six years later.

St Katharine Docks

St Katharine Docks, just east of the **Tower of London** beyond **Tower Bridge**, mark the westernmost point and start of London's **Docklands** area. These docks were designed by Thomas Telford and opened in 1828. In their heyday they imported luxury cargoes including sugar, rum, tea, spices, perfumes and marble, and were reported to have the greatest concentration of portable wealth in the world.

Following the decline and eventual closure of the once-thriving Port of London, in the 1970s St Katharine Docks became the first part of Docklands to be redeveloped. Today, old ships and luxury yachts nestle side by side in this pretty marina (which can just be seen top right of the photograph), where swing bridges add historic interest. Ivory House – built in 1852 – still stands with its distinctive clock tower, and quayside pubs, restaurants and shops in converted warehouses add to the attraction for visitors.

Tower Bridge

*T*he familiar landmark that is **Tower Bridge** gives magnificent views over London and the River Thames.

Until the late 1800s, **London Bridge** was the capital's most easterly river crossing, even though a large percentage of the population lived even further to the east. A new bridge that allowed tall ships to reach the busy Pool of London which handled cargo arriving from all corners of the globe, as well as one that would support traffic going across it, was needed. The chosen design was the work of architect Horace Jones and engineer John Wolfe Barry. This remarkable example of Victorian Gothic architecture and engineering, completed in 1894, is a bascule bridge, which allows the roadway to lift and ships to pass through.

The **Tower Bridge Exhibition** presents a history of the bridge and enables visitors to see its engine rooms, as well as views of London and the Thames from the elevated walkways.

The curved glass building seen to the right of Tower Bridge is **City Hall**, home to the offices of the Mayor of London and the London Assembly. Over the water from City Hall is the **Tower of London**.

Just beyond Tower Bridge, on the south bank, is **Shad Thames**, running behind the converted warehouses at **Butler's Wharf** where there are exclusive shops and riverside restaurants. Shad Thames itself retains much of its original character with its brickwork buildings and hanging ironwork gantries, over which dock workers once wheeled their cargo.

HMS Belfast

Upriver, on the south bank between **Tower Bridge** and **London Bridge**, are several landmarks, including **HMS** *Belfast*, seen in the foreground of the photograph. This armoured warship saw action during the Second World War; decommissioned in 1965, it now offers a floating history of the Royal Navy and a chance for visitors to explore its decks.

The City

What is officially 'The City' of London is often referred to as the 'Square Mile' (it actually measures 1.12 square miles/ 2.9 square kilometres), which centuries ago was the extent of London. The area covers a little more than that bounded by the Roman, and later medieval, walls, and extends from Temple Bar in the west (near **Somerset House**, home of the **Courtauld Gallery**) to the historic **Tower of London** in the east (in the foreground of the photograph), and from Islington in the north to the River Thames in the south.

For a long time the City has been the capital's financial district. The area was all but destroyed in the Great Fire of 1666, and the buildings seen today are a result of the Victorian era, post-Second World War construction, and – more recently – the 1980s boom, when much of the office space was built, including the controversial **Lloyds Building**. Equally fascinating, its neighbour **The Gherkin** was opened in 2004; this unique structure is centre-right of the photograph.

The green area opposite the Tower of London is **Trinity Square Gardens**. The spired church to the west of the Tower of London is **All Hallows by the Tower**; dating from AD 675, it is the oldest church in the City. Central to the City is the magnificent **St Paul's Cathedral** whose fine frontage looks towards Fleet Street, best known as the home of British newspapers until the 1980s, with the 'journalists' church' of **St Brides** and **Dr Johnson's House** nearby.

Comparatively recent additions to the City are the **Museum of London**, where visitors can unravel the history of London from its prehistoric past to the present day, and the **Barbican Centre**, Europe's largest multi-arts centre and home of the London Symphony Orchestra. A little beyond the Barbican, close to the City's northernmost boundary, is **Wesley's Chapel**, where visitors can discover the story of Methodism in the museum in the crypt, and also explore **John Wesley's House**.

St Paul's Cathedral

*E*arly on the morning of Sunday 2 September 1666, Londoners awoke to a city ablaze with a fire that was already out of hand and was to rage for four days and nights. Along with many other buildings, the Great Fire of London destroyed 87 churches – among them **St Paul's Cathedral**.

Christopher Wren was tasked with designing 51 new churches in the city, as well as a new cathedral on the site where a cathedral dedicated to St Paul had stood since AD 604. The foundation stone of New St Paul's was laid on 21 June 1675 and the building was declared formally complete in 1711. On 21 June 2011 a service of celebration was held to mark the 300th anniversary of the cathedral, on completion of a 15-year cleaning and restoration programme.

Rising majestically at the brow of Ludgate Hill, and despite encroaching tower blocks in the 20th and 21st centuries, the iconic St Paul's has stood the test of time, even surviving the Blitz of the Second World War when a total of 28 bombs landed on it.

The true glory of its magnificent dome is most fully appreciated from inside the cathedral, which is decorated with monochrome frescoes designed by Sir James Thornhill – apparently against the wishes of Wren, who had intended a mosaic interior.

The dome contains three galleries. The most well known, the Whispering Gallery, is inside the building, and is where words whispered on one side can be heard on the other, over 30m (100 feet) away. The other two galleries are outside the cathedral: visitors can climb to the Stone Gallery at the base of the dome, and a further 528 steps to the Golden Gallery which sits beneath the golden ball and cross on top of the cathedral. The panoramic views are worth the climb.

The distance from the pavement to the top of the cross is around 111m (365 feet). Below ground level, the peaceful crypt is the burial place of architect Christopher Wren, where part of the wording on a simple plaque translates as 'If you seek his monument, look around you'.

American Memorial Chapel

Behind the High Altar of **St Paul's Cathedral** is the **American Memorial Chapel**. It was built in the 1950s to commemorate the servicemen and women from the United States who were based in Britain during the Second World War, and who gave their lives during the conflict. Significantly, the chapel built on part of the cathedral destroyed during the Blitz in October 1940. It was funded by donations from the British people following an appeal launched in November 1945. The three windows in the chapel date from 1960, with a theme of service and sacrifice.

Millennium Bridge: from St Paul's to Tate Modern

Linking **St Paul's Cathedral** in the City to the north with **Tate Modern** in Bankside to the south is an elegant, modern addition to the crossings over the River Thames – the **London Millennium Footbridge**, designed by Norman Foster. This steel suspension bridge opened in June 2000, but as people streamed across the 325-m (1,066-foot) structure, its swaying motion earned it the nickname 'the wobbly bridge'. It was closed as a safety precaution for further engineering work, and reopened in February 2002.

Tate Modern

Tate Modern art gallery is the 21st-century sister to **Tate Britain** at Millbank. Tate Modern is housed in the austere building (designed by Sir Giles Gilbert Scott) that was once Bankside Power Station, converted from its industrial use in 2000. This magnificent exhibition space features some of the world's leading art collections from 1900 to the present day. Art lovers can explore exhibits over seven levels, the uppermost of which is a café with amazing views over the river.

Southwark

*I*n the shadow of **London Bridge** and central to the Borough of Southwark is **Southwark Cathedral**. This is one of London's oldest places of worship, originally built in medieval times as an Augustinian priory church, St Mary Overy ('over the river'). The monks also created St Thomas' Hospital, which moved to its present location opposite the Houses of Parliament in 1871. The **Old Operating Theatre Museum** is on the site of the old hospital. Parts of the 13th-century cathedral remain but Southwark Cathedral's magnificent nave is 19th century. An extension in 2000 has provided additional facilities to the building, with an excellent education centre, gift shop and refectory.

Just beyond the cathedral, adding cheery colour with its awnings under the railway arches, is one of London's most popular food markets – **Borough Market**. A little beyond this is the **George Inn**, the only remaining galleried coaching hostelry in London, and one that William Shakespeare is said to have frequented; it is now in the ownership of the National Trust. Also in the vicinity are two themed attractions, not for the faint-hearted: the **London Dungeon** and the **London Bridge Experience**.

West of Southwark Cathedral and on the River Thames is the *Golden Hinde*, a replica of Sir Francis Drake's Tudor galleon. Just a few metres away, in Clink Street, is the **Clink Prison Museum**, where a gaol stood until 1780.

The Shard

A 21st-century addition to Southwark's skyline is **The Shard**, which on its completion in 2012 became the tallest building in western Europe at 310m (1,106 feet). The Shard has 72 floors of office space, plus apartments, restaurants and an hotel, and a further 15 (uninhabitable) floors in the spire. A high-speed lift whisks visitors to 'The View' – an observatory on the uppermost floors, with views extending up to 64km (40 miles).

Shakespeare's Globe

Fronting **Bankside Pier** on the River Thames, and in the shadow of **Tate Modern** to its right, is **Shakespeare's Globe** theatre. This is a reconstruction of William Shakespeare's Elizabethan playhouse which stood in nearby Park Street. The original Globe burned down in 1613 – the result of an ember from a cannon, fired during a performance of *Henry VIII*, setting light to the thatched roof. It was rebuilt the following year but demolished by the Puritans in the 1640s.

The theatre seen today was the extraordinary brainchild of American movie mogul Sam Wanamaker, who died before it was completed. When it was finished in 1997, it was the first thatched building permitted to be erected in the capital since the Great Fire of London of 1666.

Many of Shakespeare's plays premiered in the original Globe, in which he was also a stakeholder – and at times an actor. Today, open-air productions can be enjoyed here in the summer months, much in the style that they would have been in the 17th century. Audio and guided tours – along with an interactive exhibition – are exciting, year-round 21st-century additions.

In keeping with Wanamaker's original intention, there are plans to build an indoor Jacobean theatre on the same site as Shakespeare's Globe. This will be a footprint of Blackfriars Theatre – also part-owned by the Bard, but situated on the other side of the river and demolished in 1655 – which staged his plays suited only to an indoor arena.

London Eye

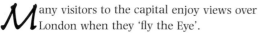

Many visitors to the capital enjoy views over London when they 'fly the Eye'.

The **London Eye** is situated on the south bank between **Westminster Bridge** and **Hungerford Bridge/Golden Jubilee Footbridge**; the latter, opened in 2002, was named in honour of the 50th anniversary of **Queen Elizabeth II's** accession.

The London Eye is a prominent landmark, erected in celebration of the new millennium and officially opened to the public in March 2000. At 135-m (443-feet) high, when it was built it was the fourth tallest structure in London and the world's largest observation wheel.

As the 32 glass pods rotate slowly over the River Thames, a half-hour ride offers panoramic views of up to 40km (25 miles) on a fine day – as far as Windsor Castle. Around 800 passengers can travel on the Eye at any one time, and around 3.5 million people take the trip each year.

Next to the London Eye is **County Hall**, opened in 1922 by George V. Inside are a number of restaurants and exhibitions. A little further to the east, towards **Waterloo Bridge**, are the **Royal Festival Hall**, the **Hayward Gallery**, **BFI Southbank** and – just beyond the bridge – the **National Theatre**.

Imperial War Museum

East of **Westminster Bridge**, the domed building at the end of Lambeth Road was once the Bethlehem Royal Hospital – 'Bedlam', a lunatic asylum – but is now home to the **Imperial War Museum**. Despite the naval guns at the entrance, this museum is much more than a display of military memorabilia, with emphasis placed on the effects of warfare on the lives of servicemen and women, and civilians, from 1914 to the present day. As well as impressive military equipment, the comprehensive collection of exhibits include moving testimonies from ordinary people affected by wartime experiences, in particular the First and Second World Wars, and interactive recreations of the sights and sounds of a war-torn London.

Lambeth Palace

*O*verlooking the River Thames, between **Westminster Bridge** and **Lambeth Bridge**, and opposite the **Houses of Parliament**, is **Lambeth Palace**. This has been the London residence of the Archbishop of Canterbury since the 13th century; the palace and its garden are open to the public on only a few days each year. Adjacent to it is **Archbishop's Park**, officially opened in 1901; it includes a site dedicated to Octavia Hill, co-founder of the National Trust and a campaigner for open spaces for all to enjoy.

Close to Lambeth Palace is the **Garden Museum**. The museum was set up in 1977 in the derelict church and grounds of St Mary-at-Lambeth. The 17th-century-themed garden celebrates two of the greatest botanical specialists of all time, John Tradescant and his son – also John – who are buried here.

Over the road from Archbishop's Park and fronting the river is **St Thomas' Hospital**, the successor of one founded by monks in Southwark in the 13th century, and where Florence Nightingale established the first school of nursing in 1859. The South Wing is seen top right of the photograph. Inside the hospital is the **Florence Nightingale Museum**, which relates the story of the founder of modern nursing and in particular her tireless work during the Crimean War. Fascinating interactive displays and exhibits include the lamp that earned Miss Nightingale her title as 'the lady of the lamp'.

Westminster

The historic beginnings and naming of the area known as **Westminster** (seen looking upriver here and downriver overleaf) focus on the former Thorney Island, a marshy place where Edward the Confessor established a palace and church – his 'west minster', which is around 3km (2 miles) from the 'east minster' (**St Paul's Cathedral**).

Westminster Bridge is one of many crossings over the River Thames in London. The current bridge dates from 1862, replacing the original 1750 structure which was built despite fierce opposition from ferrymen. Apart from **Putney Bridge** further west, Westminster Bridge was only the second one to be built in the heart of the capital: **London Bridge**, further downriver, was the sole crossing place for centuries.

Many river trips start from **Westminster Pier**, one of five new piers created in 2000 as part of the millennium project. A river cruise is a delightful, meandering way to enjoy the urban and industrial landscape of London,

as well as its greener places, or indeed its semi-rural aspects, such as **Greenwich**, **Hampton Court** and **Kew**, without being caught up in the bustle of busy streets.

Prestigious landmarks in the City of Westminster include: the **Houses of Parliament**; **Parliament Square**, with its statues of, amongst others, Winston Churchill and Nelson Mandela; **Buckingham Palace**; **Wellington Arch**; **Whitehall**, home of **10 Downing Street**, the official residence of Britain's Prime Minister; **Trafalgar Square**; the **National Gallery** and the **National Portrait Gallery**; **Westminster Abbey**; **Westminster Cathedral**; **Somerset House**; the **Savoy Hotel**; **Tate Britain**, founded in 1897 as the Tate Gallery but rechristened when **Tate Modern** opened.

In the midst of the streets, traffic and buildings of the borough, several royal parks provide peaceful oases, and include **Green Park**, **Hyde Park** and **St James's Park**.

Houses of Parliament

*O*ne of the finest sights in London is the country's seat of government – the **Houses of Parliament**, or the New Palace of Westminster as it is properly known. Seen from the River Thames, its beautiful 265-m- (872-foot-) long honey-coloured façade of pinnacles, towers and tracery is one of the most photographed sights in the capital.

Parliament consists of the **House of Commons**, which proposes new laws and questions ministers about government policies, while the **House of Lords** considers, and often amends, bills passed to it by the Commons – only after consideration by both Houses can they become law.

The origins of the building date back to the 11th century when Edward the Confessor built a royal palace here, which also served as a meeting place for Parliament. It remained the principal residence of England's kings until Henry VIII moved his royal court to Whitehall Palace and **St James's Palace**.

It was beneath Parliament Chamber in 1605 that Guy Fawkes and his co-conspirators planted barrels of gunpowder – an act of treason resulting in their execution in **Old Palace Yard**. The Gunpowder Plot was unsuccessful, but a fire in 1834 destroyed almost all of the building. The Victorian Gothic masterpiece that stands today on its 3.2-ha (8-acre) site is the work of Charles Barry and Augustus Pugin. One of the survivors of the Old Palace, however, is **Westminster Hall**, which narrowly avoided destruction during the Second World War when other parts of the building suffered bomb damage.

The distinguished **Clock Tower**, often referred to as **Big Ben**, is another of London's most photographed landmarks. Strictly speaking, it is the 13.75-tonne bell that chimes the hour that is actually Big Ben. The tower at the opposite end of the complex to the 96-m (316-foot) Clock Tower is the slightly taller **Victoria Tower** (98m/323 feet). It is from Victoria Tower that the Union Jack flies when Parliament is sitting and, at night, a light shines from the Clock Tower when either House is sitting.

Westminster Abbey

*I*n the shadow of the **Houses of Parliament**, **Westminster Abbey** manages to combine a bustling tourist destination with a quiet sense of peace for those seeking a place for reflection.

When Edward the Confessor established a royal palace and church in the west (west minster) he dedicated the church to St Peter, giving the abbey its full title: The Collegiate Church of St Peter, Westminster.

Westminster Abbey is where the coronations of all English monarchs except two have taken place since Edward the Confessor's successor, William the Conqueror, was crowned in 1066. The current church was begun by Henry III in 1245, in French Gothic style, but the building as a whole was not finished in the style seen today until 1745, when the western towers were completed.

Just beyond the north door of Westminster Abbey, shrouded by trees in this photograph, is **St Margaret's Church**. Now the parish church of the House of Commons, it was originally built as a place of worship for local people so that the occupants of the Benedictine monastery that once stood on the site of Westminster Abbey could pray undisturbed.

The domed building on the left of the photograph is the **Methodist Central Hall**. In front of St Margaret's Church is **Parliament Square**, and the road leading due north is **Whitehall,** dominated by white buildings comprising HM Treasury and the Foreign and Commonwealth Office, with **Downing Street** off to the left. Beyond is **Horse Guards**, with its parade ground visible towards the top right of the photograph; this is the headquarters of the Household Cavalry and home of the **Household Cavalry Museum**.

Westminster Cathedral

Westminster Cathedral in Victoria Street is the Mother Church of Roman Catholicism in England and Wales, and is the seat of the Archbishop of Westminster.

The cathedral was built on what at one time had been marshy ground surrounding Westminster, on a site that in the past was a fairground, a maze, a bull-baiting ring and a prison. The land was acquired by the Catholic Church in 1884.

Designed by John Francis Bentley, Westminster Cathedral was started in 1895 with its first service being held in 1903. Although the building has never actually been completed, the cathedral was consecrated in 1910.

This Byzantine-style structure is made from terracotta bricks and white Portland stone, giving it its distinctive striped appearance. It is topped with a magnificent bell tower, 83-m (273-feet) high. This campanile is dedicated to St Edward the Confessor. The viewing gallery in the tower gives spectacular 360-degree views over London.

The interior of the cathedral, with its series of chapels, is richly decorated in mosaic and marble. The nave is the highest and widest in England, and gives an uninterrupted view of the high altar. Eric Gill's magnificent Stations of the Cross (representing Jesus' journey to his crucifixion) are world famous; they were dedicated in 1918.

Buckingham Palace

At the head of The Mall sits the splendid memorial to Queen Victoria, great-great-grandmother to Queen Elizabeth II, and behind it the magnificent **Buckingham Palace**. During daylight hours it is rare to see the palace's frontage without a sea of visitors enjoying the spectacle, especially when the Changing the Guard ceremony takes place. When Her Majesty the Queen is in residence, the Royal Standard flutters from a flagpole.

Buckingham Palace has been the official London home of Britain's reigning sovereign since Queen Victoria took up residence on her accession in 1837. Buckingham House, as it was originally known, was purchased by George III from the Duke of Buckingham in 1762. The house was turned into a palace by George IV in the late 1820s, to a design by architect John Nash.

It is only since 1993 that visitors have been able to purchase tickets and tour some of the splendid State Rooms inside the palace, which happens during the summer when Her Majesty resides at her Scottish home, Balmoral. **The Queen's Gallery**, on the south side of the palace, is another delight for visitors, with magnificent artworks from the Royal Collection on display.

A little further along Buckingham Palace Road are the **Royal Mews**, where working stables housing liveried horses and royal carriages are a popular attraction – in particular the sumptuous Gold State Coach which is used for coronations.

Green Park borders Buckingham Palace to the north, while **St James's Park** is to the southeast, across The Mall from **St James's Palace** and **Clarence House**.

St James's Park

Sweeping eastwards from **Buckingham Palace** to **Downing Street** – linking Crown and State – is **St James's Park**, covering 23ha (58 acres). Central to the park is its lake, originally a canal, where the Blue Bridge provides views of Buckingham Palace in one direction and the domes and pinnacles of Whitehall in the other.

St James's is the oldest of London's royal parks. The land was enclosed by Henry VIII for hunting in 1532. Charles II opened it as a public park and it was remodelled in the 1820s by John Nash.

Just beyond the park is **Horse Guards Parade**, the stage for the Trooping the Colour ceremony. **Admiralty Arch**, leading to **Trafalgar Square**, is visible on the left of the photograph at the end of The Mall – the processional route to Buckingham Palace. On the other side of the park is Birdcage Walk, which takes its names from an aviary owned by James I. Along Birdcage Walk are the **Guards Chapel** and the **Guards Museum**.

St Paul's Cathedral is clearly visible in the distance, with **The Gherkin** off to the right. On the far right of the photograph, fronting the River Thames, is the **London Eye**.

St James's Palace and Clarence House

The red-brick gate tower is one of the remaining original Tudor features of **St James's Palace**, built by Henry VIII on the site of the Hospital of St James, an infirmary for lepers. When Whitehall Palace burned down in 1698, St James's Palace became the principal royal residence until **Buckingham Palace** took over the role when Queen Victoria came to the throne.

Right of St James's Palace is **Clarence House**, named after its first resident, the Duke of Clarence (later King William IV). It became the home of the late Queen Mother following her daughter Queen Elizabeth II's coronation in 1953. It is now the official London home of Prince Charles.

Trafalgar Square

Trafalgar Square was designed by John Nash in the 1820s, but it was architect Charles Barry who completed the layout in the 1840s. Its centrepiece, the 56-m (185-foot) **Nelson's Column**, was erected in 1843 in honour of naval hero Lord Nelson who was fatally wounded at the Battle of Trafalgar in 1805. The bronze lions at the foot of the column date from the 1860s and are by Sir Edwin Landseer. The fountains, by Sir Edwin Lutyens, are a 20th-century addition.

Behind Nelson, the area to the north of Trafalgar Square is dominated by the **National Gallery**, with the **National Portrait Gallery** situated behind. The National Gallery was originally situated in Pall Mall, but in 1831 Parliament decided to construct a new building in what was considered to be the very centre of London and it opened in 1838. The National Portrait Gallery was established in 1856, its collection started with what is known as the Chandos portrait of William Shakespeare.

Across the square to the east is **St Martin-in-the-Fields**, built in 1726 on the site of a previous church which was literally surrounded by fields. St Martin's is the parish church of **Buckingham Palace**, and a popular venue for concerts.

South-west of Trafalgar Square is the sweeping façade of **Admiralty Arch** which is the entrance to The Mall.

Charing Cross Station is another landmark nearby. The Eleanor Cross outside the station is a copy of the last of the 12 crosses erected by Edward I in memory of his wife, Queen Eleanor, who died near Lincoln while journeying to meet him in Scotland. The crosses mark the stopping places for the funeral procession on its way to **Westminster Abbey**, where she was buried. Only three original crosses remain; this replica, erected in 1865, stands a short distance from where the original once stood, on the south side of Trafalgar Square.

Covent Garden

Covent Garden is named after a convent whose fields once occupied this site, and whose produce became a major source of fruit and vegetables in London. The first licensed market was held here around 1670. For centuries Covent Garden was the principal market in the capital for fruit, vegetables and flowers until it moved out in 1974, when the area was transformed into a complex of shops, market stalls, restaurants and bars. Today's Apple Market is a reminder of those earlier times, with arts and crafts sold from pretty, old-fashioned apple carts.

The fourth Earl of Bedford commissioned Inigo Jones to turn the area into an Italian-style piazza in the 1630s. One of the remaining features of Jones' architecture is **St Paul's Church**, its portico supported by two columns and two piers (seen in the centre of the photograph). It was outside here in 1662 that Samuel Pepys witnessed the first-recorded Punch and Judy show in England, a forerunner of the eclectic mix of street entertainers who now perform in Covent Garden. Many of the buildings seen today date from around 1830, with the Victorian glass canopy a later addition. In the south-east corner of the piazza is the **London Transport Museum**, housed in what was once the flower market.

Theatreland

The area around **Covent Garden** is popularly termed 'Theatreland,' and is London's main theatre district, with around 40 venues located nearby. The **Royal Opera House** is on the site of the original Theatre Royal Covent Garden. The **Theatre Royal Drury Lane** – now the oldest theatre in London – is just a few steps away.

British Museum

Despite its name, the colonnaded **British Museum** in Bloomsbury contains a wealth of fascinating antiquities telling the history of civilizations and cultures from around the world.

The British Museum was founded in 1753 to house the collections of Sir Hans Sloane, who had offered them to the nation in his will. Its central courtyard – the Great Court, designed by Norman Foster – opened in 2000 and sits beneath a striking curved glass roof.

Nearby are some of the finest squares in London, including **Bedford Square**, **Bloomsbury Square**, where Hans Sloane had a medical practice, and **Russell Square**, where the gardens are in the style of the original 19th-century layout.

Behind the British Museum is the **Senate House**, an art-deco building that houses the library for the University of London. When it was built in 1937, it was the tallest structure in London at 64m (210 feet).

Further west of the British Museum lies the hub of London's west-end shopping streets: **Oxford Street**, **Regent Street** and **Bond Street**.

Kensington Museums

Kensington is home to three of London's best-loved visitor attractions, all within a few steps of each other: the **Victoria and Albert Museum**, the **Natural History Museum** and the **Science Museum**. The museums are built on land purchased with profits from the Great Exhibition of the Works and Industry of All Nations of 1851, a world fair that celebrated the arts, commerce and industry.

The Victoria and Albert Museum (its grand tiered entrance seen just below centre of the photograph) was founded in 1852, its aim to educate and inspire in the areas of art, design and manufacturing. During its long history, the museum has gathered an enormous number of treasures from all over the world, exhibited in an astonishing 10km (6 miles) of halls and galleries.

The neo-Gothic building over the road from the V&A is the Natural History Museum. It exhibits millions of awe-inspiring specimens – great and small – of the earth's flora and fauna from pre-history to the present day. The museum hosts a variety of exhibitions and there are different events taking place every day.

Around the corner from the Natural History Museum, there is something for everyone at the Science Museum. Founded in 1857, the museum presents its themes in an exciting and user-friendly way, with plenty of hands-on experiences. Changing exhibits in its galleries reflect the constantly advancing worlds of science, technology, industry and medicine.

The Roman Catholic **Brompton Oratory** is seen in the foreground to the right of the photograph. Less than a mile away from the museums, where Kensington meets Knightsbridge, are two of London's most prestigious and not-to-be-missed shopping experiences – **Harrods** and **Harvey Nichols**.

Kensington Palace and Gardens

Kensington Gardens cover 111ha (275 acres) and is one of London's most charming royal parks. At the heart of Kensington Gardens is **Kensington Palace**. The gardens and palace are open to the public.

Kensington Palace was a principal residence for several royal monarchs from 1689, and the birthplace of Queen Victoria. In more recent times, Diana, Princess of Wales lived in an apartment here, and the palace is still home to other members of the royal family, including the Duke and Duchess of Cambridge.

A project completed in 2012 to re-landscape the grounds opens up and reunites the palace and gardens, with the 1893 statue of Queen Victoria as its centrepiece. There are several other landmarks in Kensington Gardens, including the **Round Pond** which has a variety of fish and waterfowl; close to the Marlborough Gate entrance to the grounds, and at the head of the Long Water, are the **Italian Gardens**; a short way from here is **Peter Pan**, a statue commissioned by author J.M. Barrie of his most famous character.

The **Serpentine Bridge** provides a crossing over the lake where the Long Water in Kensington Gardens becomes the Serpentine in **Hyde Park**. Next to the bridge is the **Serpentine Gallery**, exhibiting a range of contemporary artworks.

On the south side of Kensington Gardens, facing the **Royal Albert Hall**, is the **Albert Memorial**. This glorious gilded Gothic structure was commissioned by Queen Victoria in memory of her consort, Prince Albert, who died in 1861.

Royal Albert Hall

O n the opposite side of Kensington Gore to the **Albert Memorial** (in the foreground of the photograph) and **Kensington Gardens** is another fine monument to Queen Victoria's consort – the **Royal Albert Hall**. The most imposing view of the building is from the south side, where an 1858 statue of Prince Albert looks down from a pedestal.

The Royal Albert Hall is one of London's most popular concert venues, renowned for 'the Proms' (the Henry Wood Promenade Concerts) that take place annually. At the heart of this splendid red-brick building is the beautiful auditorium, topped by an iron and glass dome.

Like the **Kensington museums**, the site on which the Royal Albert Hall stands was purchased with proceeds from the Great Exhibition of 1851. This building was a result of Prince Albert's wish to provide a versatile exhibition space for the arts and manufactured goods, and a place where scientific conferences could be held.

The death of the Prince at the age of 42 delayed the plans but his co-organizer of the Great Exhibition, Henry Cole, took over. It was Cole who championed the idea that the design of the building should reflect a Roman amphitheatre. A frieze on the outside depicts 'the Triumph of Arts and Sciences'.

The building was due to be called the Central Hall of Arts and Sciences but its name was changed to the Royal Albert Hall of Arts and Sciences by Queen Victoria, who laid the foundation stone on 20 May 1867. A 500-strong orchestra played at the opening ceremony on 29 March 1871.

A little further south is the main campus of **Imperial College**. In the middle of the site, surrounded by modern buildings, is the copper-domed 87-m- (287-feet-) tall Queen's Tower. Dating from the Victorian age it is the only remaining part of the Imperial Institute, the forerunner of the college.

Wembley Stadium

The original **Wembley Stadium** (first known as the Empire Stadium) was the centrepiece of a British Empire Exhibition that attracted 27 million visitors. The exhibition was opened by King George V on 23 April (St George's Day) in 1924.

The stadium is named after its location in north London and has long been synonymous with English football. Although not officially opened until the following year, in 1923 it hosted its first FA Cup final when Bolton Wanderers played West Ham United. The stadium's best-remembered event, however, is the 1966 World Cup final when England played West Germany, winning 4–2.

The original Wembley Stadium was demolished in 2003; the current one opened in 2007 and is once again home to England's national football team, though it is also now famed for hosting other sporting events and epic concerts. Its most striking feature is its iconic arch which is 133-m (435-feet) tall. The stadium has the longest single-span roof structure in the world, spanning 315m (just over 1,000 feet), with the sliding roof allowing the pitch to be covered or not, as the weather dictates.

Wembley Arena, opposite Wembley Stadium, was completed in 2006, renovating the original 1934 arena. It is one of London's largest indoor venues for concerts and sporting events.

Wimbledon

The world's most prestigious tennis tournament is held at Wimbledon in June each year. The 17-ha (42-acre) site is famed for its 19 grass courts (including Centre Court on the right of the photograph and No.1 Court on the left).

The All England Croquet and Lawn Tennis Club (as the club is properly known) has its beginnings in 1868, when The All England Croquet Club was founded in Worple Road, Wimbledon. In 1875 lawn tennis was introduced, which led to its renaming. The principal court was in the middle of the lawns, with other courts arranged around it – hence the term 'Centre Court'.

The world's first Lawn Tennis Championship (Gentlemen's Singles) was held at Worple Road in July 1877; in 1884 the Ladies' Singles and Gentlemen's Doubles were introduced; and by the turn of the century Wimbledon had gone international with its first overseas Champion winning in 1905. In 1922 the popularity of the sport led to the club relocating to its present home in Church Road. That same year tickets were first issued by ballot – a system continued for every Championship since. Prize money was first awarded in 1968 – the same year that professional players were first allowed to compete in The Championships. Prizes for the tournament in 1968 totalled £26,150, compared with over £14.6 million in 2011 – the 125th staging of the event; there were no Championships played during the First and Second World Wars.

Wimbledon has grown and moved with the times. The 21st century has seen the completion of – amongst other things – a museum, an increase in seating capacity and, perhaps most notably, a retractable roof installed over Centre Court.

Kew Gardens

Kew Gardens lie less than 16km (10 miles) from the centre of London. The landscaping of the grounds was started by Frederick, Prince of Wales and his wife, Princess Augusta, in the 18th century. Today the Royal Botanic Gardens, as they are properly known, welcome thousands of visitors to the largest collection of living plants in the world on this 121-ha (300-acre) site.

There are many buildings to be enjoyed at Kew but the most celebrated is the **Palm House**, west of Palm House Pond towards the top of the photograph. This masterpiece of engineering in wrought iron and glass dates from the 1840s. Its humidity mimics a tropical rainforest and an elevated walkway enables visitors to enjoy a treetop view.

The **Temperate House** (centre left), also Victorian, is the largest glasshouse at Kew and is home to plants from every continent. The **Princess of Wales Conservatory**, with its distinctive sloping roof (seen north of the pond), is named after Princess Augusta. Built in the 1980s, its climate-regulated zones enable everything from cacti to orchids to grow. A number of follies are dotted around the gardens, including the **Pagoda** (at the bottom of the photograph). This 50-m- (163-feet-) high structure was built in 1762.

Also in the grounds of Kew Gardens is the red-brick **Kew Palace**, close to the River Thames and open to the public at certain times of year. Built *c.*1631, it was purchased by George III in 1781.

Hampton Court Palace

South-west of London, on the banks of the River Thames, is the vast Tudor estate of **Hampton Court Palace** with its 26.7-ha (66-acre) garden. Each July this is the venue for the Hampton Court Palace Flower Show – the world's largest event of its kind.

There has been a manor at Hampton since the 13th century, but it was Cardinal Wolsey who built a vast bishop's palace here in the early 16th century. Hampton Court Palace came into Henry VIII's ownership in 1528 when Wolsey fell from favour. Henry's additions to the building include the Great Hall, with its spectacular hammer-beam roof, and the enormous Tudor kitchens, large enough to feed 600 people. The Haunted Gallery is where the ghost of Catherine Howard (Henry VIII's fifth wife) is said to scream her innocence at the accusation of adultery, for which she was beheaded in 1542.

Soon after William and Mary came to the throne in 1689 the royal couple had large sections of the palace remodelled by Christopher Wren. His transformation included replacing Tudor towers and chimneys with the elegant baroque exteriors that today front the formal gardens.

The main entrance to the palace is via the Great Gatehouse, seen on the far left of the photograph, which leads into the open courtyard and Clock Court beyond. To the east of the building is the semi-circular Great Fountain Garden; leading to the river on the south side is the intricate Privy Garden, re-created to William III's design of 1702.

Hampton Court Palace has not been lived in by a reigning monarch since George II died in 1760, but in 1838 the young Queen Victoria ordered that it 'should be thrown open to all her subjects without restriction'.

Hampton Court maze

Hampton Court Palace's maze (just seen top left in the main photograph, to the left of the white Lion Gate) has puzzled royalty and tourists for over 300 years. It was laid out in around 1700 to provide courtiers with an escape from the politics of palace life, and is the oldest surviving hedge maze in Britain.

Windsor Castle

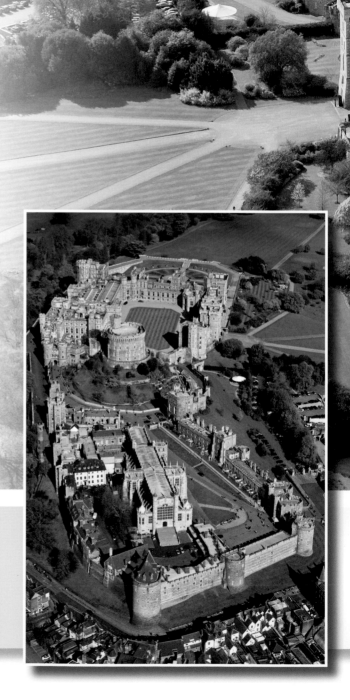

The splendid towers and ramparts of **Windsor Castle** (seen here from the east side) rise over the River Thames and the town of Windsor, just 32km (20 miles) from London.

The original castle was founded by William the Conqueror *c*.1080. Since the time of Henry I, Windsor Castle has been used by a succession of monarchs; it is one of the official residences of Her Majesty Queen Elizabeth II and the largest inhabited castle in the world.

The **Round Tower** crowns the Middle Ward in the centre of the complex, with the Lower Ward to the south-west and the Upper Ward to the east, bordered by the formal gardens of the East Terrace (seen in the foreground of the main photograph). Visitors can explore various areas of the castle, some only at certain times of the year.

Following an extensive restoration programme, it is difficult to imagine the devastation caused by the fire that ravaged over 100 rooms of the castle in 1992, including the splendid State Apartments (seen here to the right of the Upper Ward) which display some of the finest works of art from the Royal Collection.

Windsor Castle is set in 10ha (26 acres). The **Home Park** (265 ha/655 acres), south-east of the castle, is where Queen Victoria and Prince Albert are buried in the mausoleum at Frogmore. Covering 2,300ha (5,700 acres), **Windsor Great Park** stretches south of the castle, with the straight, tree-lined Long Walk a 4.8-km (3-mile) route from the George IV gate (seen left of the Upper Ward) to the Copper Horse, a statue of George III on horseback.

St George's Chapel

In the Lower Ward of **Windsor Castle** is **St George's Chapel** (the main building in the foreground of the inset photograph), one of the finest examples of late-Gothic architecture in England.

The College of St George and the Order of the Garter were founded in 1348 by Edward III. In 1475 Edward IV commissioned the building of a new chapel and St George's Chapel was completed in 1528. It is the final resting place of several monarchs, including Henry VIII who requested that he be buried 'midway between the stalls and the high altar, with the body of my true and loving Queen Jane'. The historic pageant of the Order of the Garter takes place each June, when the sovereign and Knights Companion process through the Upper, Middle and Lower Wards of the castle to the Great West Door of St George's Chapel. A service takes place in the chapel and any new Knights Companions are installed.

Eton College

The towns of Eton and Windsor are separated by the River Thames. At the end of Eton High Street – lined with independent retailers, including art and antique shops, plus pubs and restaurants – is **Eton College**, one of Britain's oldest schools. Parts of the college are open to visitors for pre-arranged guided tours.

In 1440 Henry VI founded 'The King's College of Our Lady of Eton beside Windsor', with an aim to give free education to 70 poor scholars and choristers. Today's privileged students number around 1,300, most of whom enter the school at the age of 13 and stay for five years, under the care of a housemaster, dame, dame's assistant and other staff. Each boy has his own study-bedroom and wears the traditional school dress, which includes a formal tailcoat.

The domed building in the foreground of the photograph, on the west side of Eton High Street, is School Library,

and next to it is School Hall. On the opposite side of the High Street, and at the heart of the ancient buildings of Eton College, is School Yard. To the south is the beautiful 15th-century **Eton College Chapel**. Its magnificent medieval wall paintings are some of the finest in Europe. The impressive fan-vaulted ceiling and much of the stained glass date from the 1950s, the windows a replacement for those destroyed by a bomb during the Second World War. On the north side of School Yard is Lower School, the first classroom to be built, and to the west is Upper School, built in the 17th century.

The archway of Lupton's Tower (at the head of School Yard) leads to the Cloisters, to the far left of which is Head Master's Yard; further left can be seen the edge of College Field. The building to the right beyond Lupton's Tower houses the **Museum of Eton Life**, which illustrates the life and history of the college from its founding to the present day.